I AM Healed

How A Broken Woman Found Her Purpose

Written by Tasha Moneek

ISBN-13: 978-1-7366962-4-8

Publisher's Note

Dedication

To my mom, I love you and so proud of the woman you became. I'm grateful for all the times we shared, and I forgive you. Thank you for loving me unconditionally.

To my dad, I love you and forgive you. Thank you for trying the best way you knew how too.

To my children, I'm sorry for any hurt I have caused you. I love each one of you with everything in me. And I'm proud of you guys. Maleek I'm so proud of the man you have become without having an example of a man around. Don't change who you are. Keep being the sweet low-key person that don't bother nobody you. I love that you are different. Keshawn, I know you took it hard when nana left and I know she is so very proud of you, just as I am. I see the hurt you deal with, and I wish I could bear the pain for you. But just know God did not bring you this far for no reason. Keep him first and he will never leave you. I love you and I'm very proud of you. Nevaeh God gave you to me at a time he knew I would need you more than you needed me. Nana always called you her angel and truth is you were all of our angels. You have helped me during times I was hurting the most with just a simple hug, kiss or I love you mommy. You are a tough cookie just like your mom. I cannot wait to see what God has in store for each of you. I just pray I'm here to witness it.

To my friends and family, thank so much for being supportive throughout my journey in life and with my book launch. I appreciate each one of you and love you all.

To anyone that I have hurt while I was hurting, I want to say I am sorry.

To anyone who has helped me in any way whether you allowed me to live with you or helped me in any way thank you so much.

Last but definitely not the least I want to thank God for carrying me through when I couldn't carry myself or understand why I had to go through certain things. Thank you for covering me and my family and never leaving our side. I owe everything to you for sure. I don't know about y'all God but mine come through every time.

Contents

I Am Healed

Chapter 1

Lonely

"We either make ourselves miserable, or we make ourselves strong. The amount of work is the same."

– *Carlos Castaneda*

From the time I was a little girl, I have always felt alone. I grew up having to stay with different family members because my mom battled with drug addiction. That feeling of being lonely never left as an adult. I have made some friends that I consider family but no matter how much love they showered me with, it still didn't make me feel connected to anyone. They still had their own blood family that they had gatherings with or went on family trips with. And to be honest, I envied that a little. I felt mad, well not mad but angry because I never had that experience of bonding with my family.

By the time my mother got clean and stable, I was grown and had two children. While I wish that we could have bonded in my earlier years, we had many great times that we shared together. That's when I was able to experience **REAL** family time. I used to cook for her all the time. Her favorite food was seafood, so I cooked that every year for her birthday.

Let me take a step back.

I was brought into this world by two strong people. My parents are who I get my strength from. Anybody who knew my dad knew that he did not play. I remember my friends used to say, "Your dad looks mean" and he really did. And I as a little girl felt the same way. Now, as I have become an adult, I can relate to how he did not take any mess. When life presents you with different experiences, it can sometimes cause you to have your guard up or seem to be mean, bitter, or hateful. I do not blame him for how he was. And he was not as mean as he looked.

When I lived with him during my teenage years, I remember going on his second job with him. He delivered newspapers on the weekends. He worked a full-time job and did the paper route as a part time job. So, he would be so tired from working at his fulltime job at Napa State Hospital and would ask me to go with him on his paper route. I did not mind helping him. We would roll the papers at the warehouse where he picked the newspapers up from and I would ride with him and hand him the papers to throw as he drove from house to house. When he would be driving to different areas in Fairfield, CA, he would talk to me and ask questions such as how school was. He would try to crack jokes. During this time is where I got to really see him outside of his portrayed hard shell.

Then, there was my mom; someone whom I loved so much. She was a very strong woman. Anybody who met or knew my mom loved her. She was very outspoken. But she would give you the shirt off her back. She gone talk mess in the process, but she would give her last to the people she loved. She gave tough love and didn't back down from it.

My mom and dad both battled with drug addiction most of my childhood. At times, I couldn't reside with either of them, so I'd stay with relatives. Some relatives would treat me like the stepchild, making me feel more alone. I'd overhear them talk badly about my mom being a crackhead. Of course, they would never say it to her face. But being so young, it made me hate and resent those people during that time.

I didn't care what she did. No matter what, she was still my mom and I loved her so much regardless of her addiction. Funny thing: some of the same people who talked negatively about her were using drugs then... and now.

Back & Forth

Since my mom couldn't take care of me, I was between houses a lot. My aunt's house is the first home I remember bouncing to. I have a lot of good memories of when I lived with my aunt, who is my mom's oldest sister. She never made me feel uncomfortable. She loved me like I was her own daughter. She only had one child, and I know it may have been difficult for my cousin to have to share her mom with me, especially, since it was only them for so long. But me living with my aunt only made me and my cousin closer. She protected me like her little sister. I lived with them from the age of 7 to about 10.

Next, my dad's. He finally got his life together and became the father, husband, and brother that he was meant to be. He picked me up from my aunt's and took on the role as father. I was happy to be with my dad, but I still missed my mom, who was in prison at the time.

While I was grateful to be with my dad, all I wanted was to be with my mother. I was angry with my dad because I felt like he was taking me from her. He used to ask me, "Why would you want to go be with your mom? She's not stable." Then there was a time when my mom and dad were going through a custody battle over me. I remember I had to meet with this lady by myself every week. The lady would ask me questions such as who I wanted to live with, and why I didn't want to stay with my dad. I had to meet with that lady for weeks. I remember crying saying I wanted to live with my mom. And I didn't care if she didn't have her own house. My dad would question me after every meeting. He would ask "What did you talk about and what did you say?" I can remember him being so frustrated with not understanding why I wanted to go somewhere and not have stability. I was a child so at those moments, being in a stable environment didn't really matter to me. I just wanted to be wherever my mom was. My mom and dad were scheduled for their last court date to determine the final judgement for custody. When I came home from school, I noticed that my dad was home. He came to my room, and he said "Well, I went to court today, and the judge gave me custody." At that moment, my heart dropped. Then he said, "The judge was going to grant your mom custody today, but she didn't show up to court." I was so heart broken when he said those words to me. All I could think at that moment was *Did she really not want me? Does she love me? Why didn't she show up?* At that point, I was in tears and felt like my heart was ripped from my chest. I didn't understand.

Now that I am older, I understand that my mom was battling things from her past that led to her becoming an addict. It was a temporary numb to whatever she was battling. Soon after that court hearing, my mom ended up going back to prison for a few years. I guess I was going to stay with my dad one way or another.

Feeling Unwanted

I've never felt wanted growing up. I've always felt like leftovers. Like a burden. And it trips me out that adults are so heartless to motherless and fatherless kids and will actually make them feel unwanted. That was my experience.

One night, prior to living with my dad, I remember being woken up out of my sleep because of the screaming and arguing that was happening. I was asleep in the bed with my mom's god sister. One of my mom's god sister's boyfriend was living there at the time as well. My mom was tripping again, and she just left me there. He was having it. Apparently me being there caused a huge argument because they started to fight. For whatever reason, he did not want me there. So, one of the ladies told me to get my stuff so she could take me to her mom's house for the night.

I was crushed. I heard everything they were arguing about. And every time I've had to live with other people, I've never felt like I belonged. My worst fear became to be somewhere that I was not welcomed. I wish my mom would have just taken me with her when she left so that I didn't have to be where I was not wanted.

Tainted Innocence

My mom being unstable hurt me in more ways than one. Because we bounced from house to house and my mother wasn't in her right frame of mind, she wasn't really aware of the people we were around. And because of this, my aunt's child's father touched me inappropriately. I'll never forget it. He tainted the innocent little girl within me, and it took me a while to heal from that. I trusted this guy. Even called him uncle. He'd take me to school sometimes and I'd be excited because I knew he'd drive fast, and the music would be loud. Plus, I knew he'd get me some candy.

Well, what used to be an innocent ride turned very traumatic. On this one particular day, he came to pick me up from school and was looking weird and asking me weird questions, like if anybody had ever touched me before. I looked at him and I said, "No."

Thereafter, I started to get nervous because he didn't take the usual route home. He ended up pulling up somewhere in an open field where nothing or nobody was. He continued to question me and at this point, I was scared and crying. He told me to pull my pants down. He said that if I told anybody, they would get hurt and I would get in trouble. I was sitting in the seat bawling my eyes out. "I don't want to pull them down," I said. He then pulled them down and started touching my private parts while I was still crying. He then told me that I better not tell anybody. He took me to the store and bought me candy and told me to dry my face before he took me back to the house. When we pulled up to my aunt's house, he told me to go to the bathroom to wash my face. I remember going in the bathroom and just crying my eyes out. From that point on, I never wanted him to drop me off; neither did I go anywhere with him.

My mom was not there on the day that it happened and none of my aunts even paid attention to me to notice any change in me. Even when I cried not to go with him, they would get mad and yell and make me go. They just assumed that I was going through the motions because my mom was gone.

As an adult now, I always pay attention to my kids around people; whether it's family, close friends, or their father. And I ask them questions like, "Has anyone ever tried to touch you or anything?" And they can tell me no matter if they say that they will hurt me or them. And I don't care who it is. I let them know that it's okay to tell, because as a child, I didn't tell anyone. The only person I was comfortable telling was my mom and she was nowhere to be found.

When I moved with my dad at the age of 10, he called me downstairs one day and asked me if anyone had ever touched me before. At that moment, my body just froze. I had buried that nightmare but when I heard those words come from my dad, it instantly replayed in my head.

Once I snapped out of it, I looked down and told him no. He looked at me and said, "Tasha, you can tell me if someone has ever touched you." I then told him that my aunt's kids' father had touched me before when I was staying with my other aunt. He asked if my mom knew, and I told him, "No she did not." Before he called me downstairs, I heard the TV playing and it was some talk show and they were talking about something like if your child pulls back from you when you try to be affectionate or hug them, then it could be because something has happened to them. I can't remember the exact words, but they were basically saying that maybe the child has been molested and that's why they react in that way when they are shown affection.

My dad was not a very affectionate person, but he did try to be sometimes to me and my sister. Whenever he would try to hug me, I would be very tense. Not realizing it but he did and that was the reason he asked me those questions. I could see the pain and hurt in his eyes after I told him. I'm sure he was mad at himself for not knowing sooner or not being able to protect me. I know as a mother now that I try to protect my kids as much as I can. I get on their nerves with being so observant of everything that they do. I watch how their body language is and how they interact with everyone they come in contact with; only because of what I have been through. I always say I don't understand how some people don't know when their kids are being molested while living in the same household. Not judging anyone but I don't care if I'm dating a man, I still have and will question my children at any moment. Even if they don't give me any signs, I'm still very cautious because most times, it's always someone closest to you.

This situation has most definitely affected my relationships with men. Before writing this book, I had placed that memory so far back in my mind because I just did not want to relive it. But I can say that getting it out has been a mixture of emotions for me. It brought up so many feelings. I was hurt, broken and I needed a sense of healing.

Ways to Heal Loneliness:

- *Accept that needing someone is not a sign of weakness*
- *Weed out toxic people and stick with relationships that inspire you*
- *Solitude can be valuable and enjoyable when you use it to create space to think. It can help you know yourself better and see your qualities and strengths much clearer.*

Chapter 2

Broken

"He heals the brokenhearted and binds up their wound's"

- *Psalms 147: 3*

At the age of 17 years old, I lost my father to suicide. I remember everything that led to that dreadful day like it was yesterday. Prior to his death, I had moved in with my grandmother. I wasn't getting along with him and my stepmom. I felt like the black sheep in the family. I was always getting in trouble for silly things. And I started running away.

On The Run

The very first time that I ran away, I called my auntie Val, who raised me prior to me moving with my dad. She came to Fairfield to pick me up and brought me back to her house in Vallejo. I begged her not to send me back to my dad's house, so she brought me to her house. I had gotten in trouble with my stepmom that day because one of my friends had stopped by my house to pick up her shirt. My friend had asked me to hold her shirt while we were at school, and she forgot to get it from me. So, since she lived right around the corner from me, she stopped by my house on her way home to get it. My stepmom was outside in the garage doing something and she called me out there and said my friend wanted her shirt. So, I got the shirt out of my backpack and brought it outside. When my friend left, my stepmom asked why I had her shirt. And I told her, "She asked me to hold it on our lunch because she didn't have her backpack and she didn't want to go to her locker." I guess my stepmom thought I was lying and said my friend was a snotty nose little girl and that she was going to tell my dad. This was the first time she ever saw or met this friend. Anybody that knew my stepmom and dad knew that they were very strict. I guess my stepmom thought the shirt was stolen or something. I don't know but the shirt was not new, and you could tell that it had been worn. It was a white undershirt. So, she did call my dad at work, and he said I was in trouble. That meant that I was going to get questioned over and over again about something that I was telling them the truth about. Then he was going to either whoop me or I was going to be on punishment for weeks. I was so sick of getting in trouble based on her assumptions, so I ran away.

My stepmom and sister left to go somewhere, and I left right after them. I walked around the corner to the friend's house that I got in trouble about. I wanted to use her phone to call my aunt. So, she took me to her house until my dad picked me up. She did call him and let him know that she had me. My dad was upset that she took me to her house instead of taking me home. No one was at my house because my dad was at work and my stepmom was gone. And I really didn't want to go back there.

My aunt had this machete that she kept behind her bed. When my dad was talking crazy before he came, she made sure that she had that machete sitting on her living room table when he came to pick me up. When he came, he didn't cause a scene. I knew he was mad because I had run away, and he had to pick me up from Vallejo when he got off and he worked in Napa, and we lived in Fairfield. I got in the car with him, and he said I was getting a whooping and I was on punishment. I already knew the routine, though.

I had gone to visit my mom for the weekend, and she had given me some money to go to the store while I was there with her. I didn't tell my dad or stepmom once I got back home with them, that I had money. I didn't think I had to. My cousin, Lesh, had asked me if I could go to the game that we were having that Friday. I asked my dad if I could go, and he said yes, which was a shock to me because normally, he didn't allow me to do anything. It was the day of the game and I had to wash the dishes before I could go to the game. And my stepmom had walked in the kitchen and asked me what was in my pockets. I had the money that my mom had given me, which was just a few dollars and some change. I responded and said nothing; she got so mad and said, "Take whatever is in your pockets out." So, I took the money out of my back pocket, and she asked why I lied, and I said I didn't know. She called my dad and told him that I lied about having money. My dad made her put me on the phone and asked where I got the money from, and I told him that I got it from my mom when I was with her. He then told me that I couldn't go to the game. I was so mad because I should have just said that my mom gave me money, but I knew it was still going to be an issue regardless of if I told the truth then.   My stepmom was already planning to leave. And I had it planned in my mind that when she leaves, I'm leaving this house, too. And then I ran away a second time but this time, I was gone for days, and my dad did not know where I was. I believe this time; he really knew I hated staying there.

While I was gone, I would call, and he would say just please come home so we can talk. Back then, we had pay phones. And that's how I called him so that he could not track the number down. It was right before school started of my junior year. I remember because when I left, I took all of my new school clothes; it was about three outfits. I have no idea why I even took the clothes because had I stayed gone until school started and went to school, he would have come there or had the police there to pick me up.

I remember going back home and all my clothes that were previously hanging up in the closet were on my bed as if waiting to be packed up. My dad did talk to me and asked if I wanted to be there, and I told him, "No. I don't want to live there." He didn't say anything, and I was shocked because normally, he would get so mad and then I would most likely get a whooping because I told him how I felt. This time, he didn't do that, though. He said he loved me and asked if I wanted to stay with my grandmother, which is his mom. Of course, I said yes, I knew he was not going to let me go live with my mom. So that option to me was better than living there at his house. My dad was never home anyways so I would be there with his wife, which at that moment; I didn't want to be there with her. Not long after I came back home, maybe a day or two, I ended up moving with my Grandmommy. She lived across town from my dad so he could drop in on me anytime. And I still continued going to the same school that I went to when I lived with him.

The Shift

After I left, everything went downhill. Some months after I moved out, my dad and stepmom started having issues. My dad ended up coming to stay at my grandma's house as well. He told me he was staying there until his wife moved out of the house that they had bought. And once she moved out that he and I would be moving back in. From what I gathered, once I moved out, his wife had started seeing another man, which would have been easy once I left because my dad worked all day and night, so he was hardly ever home. My sister was younger then so his wife could maneuver it very easily. It all made sense when I came home the last time I ran away, and she had all my stuff packed and ready to go.

It really shocked me because this is a person who preached about disobedience and lying all the time to me. So, to know she was having an affair blew my mind. This is someone who was in church every Sunday speaking in tongues, catching the Holy Ghost. And yes, I know now that **NOBODY** is perfect, and we all fall short. And I don't know what things she was battling at the time so I'm not here to judge. There are so many women fighting battles that we know nothing about. She could have been at her breaking point — I don't know.

However, in my eyes, she was a fraud.

Forever Changed

July 3rd my dad had come to my grand-mommies house. I was leaving that night to go stay with my aunt because we were going to Great America for the 4th of July. My dad sat me down and told me that he loved me and no matter what to follow in God's footsteps. He asked me to promise him that I would graduate from high school. At the time, I knew he was going through his situation with his wife. So, I just thought he was reassuring me that he loved me. I didn't think much of his speech.

The next day, I was hanging out with my cousin at Great America. We had so much fun. Later that night, my aunt's phone rang. It was a house phone, so, if someone called super late, something was wrong.

When I heard the phone ring, my stomach was immediately filled with knots. The first thing that popped in my head was something had happened to my mom. My aunt answered the phone and I heard her say, "Oh my God!"

At that moment, I knew whatever it was it was, was not good. My aunt or my cousin called my name, and I instantly felt my heart beating so fast. I walked down the hallway to my aunt's room and that's when she told me that my dad had passed away.

I feel like my world just crashed.

All I could do was cry myself to sleep. I had so many questions that I needed answered. Later on, down the line, my sister and I were able to talk. And that day that I had with my dad before the 4th of July, he had also had a talk with my sister. And basically, he was telling us goodbye. I didn't want to believe that my dad had committed suicide when I was younger. I was in denial, but he did.

As I became an adult and dealt with life experiences, I could see how someone may want to give up; especially when they felt alone or had no one to talk to. My dad had put his wife before his family because a lot of them did not care for her. So, he made a choice to love his wife as any man should. But once things had changed in their relationship, he probably felt like everyone would say, "I told you so." My dad was a good man. He loved his family even those he was not around on a daily basis. If you called him, he would come and help if you needed it. But he was also a man who took no shit as well.

New Life, New Lessons

So, this young girl was now fatherless and still searching for the love that she yearned for in her parents. I appreciate the seven years that I was able to have with him. And being able to experience stability and living in a family-oriented household.

Shortly after my dad's funeral, I ended up moving with my mom to Vallejo and we stayed with her god sister. And I was able to go to school there where I attended Vallejo High. I had already known some people from before; when I lived in Vallejo with my dad and then I moved into the house that my dad bought in Fairfield. I also had cousins who went to my new high school. I missed my friend whom I had at Fairfield High, but I was so happy to be able to live with my mom. I didn't mind transferring schools.

During this time, I was able to hang out with my favorite cousin, Greg. He treated me like he was my big brother even though I was the oldest. When I stayed with my auntie Val, she would get him so that we could hang out. But once I left her house, we did not see each other. We hadn't seen each other since before I was 10 and at this time, I was 17 and he was 16. It was the summer going into our senior year when I moved back. We were so happy to be reunited and going to the same school. One thing about him was that he was overprotective of me. He did not let any of his homeboys talk to me. And if they did, he would be ready to fight. It was one particular day when he had come over to my auntie house to check on me, but he had a slim dark-skinned boy with him. He introduced us and was like, "This is my pretty cousin, Tasha, I was telling you about." His friend spoke and said, "Was sup?" I remember him smiling and all I saw was a gold tooth shining. I remember thinking to myself, *My cousin never brought his homeboys around me.*

We had all kicked it and were just chilling and talking. We came to find out that my mom knew his mom and family. I was dating someone at the time we met so I did not look at my cousins' friend like that. But later on, my cousin told me that he brought him because he knew he would like me, and he did. The person I had dated ended up dumping me when we started school. He wanted me to move back to Fairfield because I was getting too much attention at VHS since I was the new girl. He was from Vallejo and went to Vallejo High. So, since I didn't move, he dumped me in between passing period. I wasn't upset anyway because a relationship was the last thing on my mind. I had just lost my father, so I didn't really even care. Plus, my cousin, Greg's homeboy had classes with me, and I could tell that he liked me. He always made sure that I was straight, and he always talked to me in class.

Even then, I really wasn't even worried about a relationship still. Somewhere in between starting my 12th grade year, I ended up moving with my cousin Greg and my auntie Vicky in the crest. My mom was clean for a short while when she picked me up after my dad passed but she ended up relapsing and she went to jail.

So, I moved in with my aunt so that I could finish my senior year. Greg and his homeboy were best friends, and his homeboy would be at his house all the time. They would be in the garage smoking or just chopping it up and Greg would call me out there. We would just be talking about everything. That's when I saw that his homeboy was a sweetheart and very respectful.

My mom fell in love with him from the time she had met him. Soon after we started school, we started dating and we took care of ourselves. I used to get a check every month from my dad after he passed. And that is how I survived while I was in high school. I had to buy everything on my own. From my clothes, food anything I needed was all on me. But we made sure that we both were straight; what I didn't have, he provided and vice versa. Both of our parents were on drugs. So, we were in survival mode. He was my first true love. Boys used to come up to me in school and ask me "Why you with that Black ass nigga?" But it was just the way he carried himself that caused me to fall in love with him. And anyone who knew him fell in love with him. My mom did and there wasn't anything that anybody could say about him; she would cuss you out about him.

We both were natural hustlers due to the environment that we grew up in. I sold dime bags to make sure that I had everything I needed during my senior year in high school. Like I said, my check from my dad wasn't much so when that ran out before the month was over, I still had to eat. From the time my dad passed, I had to raise myself financially.

Losing my father led to me experiencing my season of brokenness. Because I didn't have the paternal love, I found myself making decisions from a place of lack. It'll be years before I heal this area of my heart, but I have to admit it was worth the wait.

Ways to Heal Brokenness:

- *When we are broken, we are open and more willing to listen to God*
- *God uses this moment to reveal defects in our character, that would otherwise be difficult to see.*

- *You find beauty in brokenness when you choose to sit with him (God) and pour out all our pain and struggles, knowing he is listening to each word.*

Chapter 3

Heartache

"An important aspect of the healing of the soul is finding the courage to move beyond our pain."

— Unknown

Growing up, all I wanted was to be loved and accepted. Since I didn't have my mother and father consistently in my life, I was just searching for a love similar to that. I ended up having my first child at 19 years old, looking for familial love in my boyfriend. Definitely wasn't a part of my plan. I went to the doctor to get on birth control and before they put you on any form of birth control, they make you take a pregnancy test. Well, I took the test, and it came back positive. I was shocked as hell when the doctor said I was pregnant because I honestly had no idea that I was pregnant. All I remember thinking was, *What the hell did I just do?* I was scared and nervous.

I was fresh out of high school and had just moved in with my boyfriend at his parents' house at the time. It was a little crowded at my grandma's, so I took the offer to move in when it was extended to me. Now, we had our own separate rooms, so we didn't get pregnant in their home. After getting my due date, I realized I was already pregnant when I moved in with his family.

I called him once I got back to his house to tell him the news. He was just as shocked as I was. We were both young and this was going to be both of our first child. I had no idea about being a mom. I always told myself that if I had kids, nobody else would have to raise them. And they would not ever have to grow up without me. Because I knew how it felt to not have my parents growing up. I ended up getting really close with my child's father's family. They were family oriented. And since it was something that I always craved, it was easy for me to let my guard down and accept them like my family.

When we told his parents that I was pregnant, they took me and the baby in as if I was theirs. They knew how rough my upbringing was and they just encouraged me that raising a child can be done. His mom had seven children and she also had them young; so, she was not telling me anything that she had not been through. This reassured me that I too can be a good mom, despite being so young.

I knew from that point on that it was no longer about Tasha; it was now about my unborn child. Having my first son shaped me into the women that I am today. My son's father had no idea about being a father either. His mom was married to his stepdad and his biological father was alive, but they were not that close. All I knew was that I had to learn as I go with being a mother. I love to read so I would buy those pregnancy books and watched Baby Story all the time, which was a show that showed different births and from the beginning of birthing to the delivery. I was so intrigued with watching that show because this was my first child, and I didn't know what to expect.

My due date was at the end of March, but I ended up being two weeks overdue. I ended up having to get induced. I was induced on a Monday and delivered my son on a Wednesday via C-Section because his heart rate started dropping due to me being in labor for so many days. His father was in the operating room when I had him and I was appreciative for that. While we tried to do the family thing, it just wasn't working out. And you know what? That's okay.

Becoming A Single Mom

In the beginning of our relationship before our son was conceived, we were inseparable. When he would go hangout with his homeboys most of the time, he would want me to come with him. One time, I had gone out with one of his sisters a few months after I had our son. I went to pick my son up the next day from his other sister's house that had watched him that night. We were both still living at his mom's house, and he wasn't home when I got back from the club that night.

Red flag.

So, on my way to his sister's house, I spotted his car at these apartments. I called him before I was on my way to get my son and he said he was on his way home. When I saw his car, I knew he was at another female's house. I was pissed!

I went to get my son and I drove back that same route to see if he was still there. And he was. I felt myself getting angrier because I knew he was full of shit. I know I should have went home, but the way my feelings were set up, I did what I felt I needed to do. I pulled up to the lady's house. I parked my car right in front of her door. I got out and knocked hard. The lady's sister answered the door. When she opened it, she stood back and pulled the door open. There he was standing in the hall, holding a baby, looking crazy as hell.

Oh, I hope you don't think I stopped at the door?

Because I didn't.

I went in. I said, "How the fuck you over here being captain save a hoe with somebody else child, but you are not even at the house taking care of your own?" He just stood there and didn't say anything. He was looking like a lost puppy.

I knew going to someone's house was disrespectful but at that moment, I was so hurt and mad that I didn't care. This particular female and her group of friends were known to jump people. But at that point, I really didn't even care if that was going to be the outcome. I know I should not have brought my son with me in that moment. But he was in the car, and I could see him while I was at the door. I was young and I had an "I don't give a fuck" attitude then.

That's what heartache will do. Have you out in these streets looking crazy. Thank God for growth!

I ended up leaving after I said what I had to say. I was so hurt because this is someone who I thought loved me and wouldn't hurt me. This was a female that I knew of. We weren't friends, but she knew that I was with him. She also used to braid my hair on several occasions before I was pregnant and during my pregnancy. She even came to my baby shower!

So, I felt betrayed. And I had a feeling that they were messing around but I could never find the proof. But this day confirmed it. I used to ask him because he and his homeboys used to hang at her house sometimes. But he would say, "Oh my boy mess with her friend and we just be over there kicking it and smoking." My intuition told me otherwise and it was definitely correct.

Eventually he came back home, crying, trying to apologize. At that point, I didn't want to hear anything he had to say because had I not found out, he wasn't going tell me. So now he was caught, he wanted to be sorry, and I didn't care about his stupid tears. He got the silent treatment from me for weeks, and he continued to try to make up for it. Of course, I ended up allowing him back. Hey, I was in love.

We as women put up with more than we should. When you're not aware of your worth or your role as a woman, you allow some man to diminish your worth. So glad I've mastered that lesson.

And The Drama Begins

The cheating continued and I ended up moving out of his mother's house into my own apartment. I allowed him to come over a few times but at this point, we were not together. I got sick of him and the lies. He would blow up my phone and I would ignore his calls. He didn't want me, but of course he didn't want anyone else to have me either.

One day, he got a ride from his stepdad and got dropped off at my house. He was knocking and I just ignored him. I saw him through the slits of the window, he was acting like a fool outside. I got in my bed to lie down. I then turned around and he was standing next to my bed. He had slid each slat to window out and climbed through my kitchen window. I called his mom's house and told them that they better come get him or else I was calling the police. I was tired of his shit and him thinking he could just pop up whenever he wasn't on his cheating spree. His stepdad said that my child's father told him that I knew he was coming, which was a lie. My child's father knew I wasn't even answering any of his calls. But in order to get to me to see if I had company or just to get on my nerves, he decided to just catch a ride to my house without my permission.

Embracing My Role

As a new mother, I had no idea on how to be a mother or raise a child because as far as I can remember, my mother was mostly not consistent in my life. One thing that I always told myself was that if I ever had children, I would never allow them to feel the pain of not having their mother around and letting someone else raise them. I knew when I had my son that I would do everything in my power to keep that promise to him and give him things I did not get. Having my son, I was able to experience an unconditional, unquestionable love that I never knew even existed. My son was my first true love. I was a young mother that was in search of love trying to raising a baby.

When I used to live with my son's Memo (paternal grandmother), she would help with him so much. When I came home from the hospital, I remember my son would not stop crying. I had fed him and changed his diaper. I was so overwhelmed because I could not figure out what was wrong. I had a c-section, so I was still in a little bit of pain from that. And my room was upstairs near his memo and dad's room. So, climbing those stairs was no joke. His Memo then came to check on what was going on because Maleek had woke her up with his crying. She asked me how many scoops of milk I was putting in for his bottle. I remember telling her one scoop. She immediately said 'MAE," which was the nickname she had for me. "That isn't enough for his 6oz bottle; this baby is hungry."

I had no idea that I was supposed to put three scoops. I had brought home the formula that I received from the hospital, which was already premade. We both busted out laughing because I had been starving my poor baby. And my son was a healthy baby; he weighed 9'lbs so he was not coming to play when it came to his food. I tell him that story all the time.

Grateful for Support

Memo was a big help to me and my son. She always has treated me like her daughter even before I had her grandson. There was a time when my mom needed somewhere to go, and she even allowed her to stay the night there. She knew the many struggles I faced. She knew the struggle of raising kids; she had six kids of her own. And she has faced many adversities as well. I looked up to her as a role model. She never gave up the fight and God blessed her beyond measures.

Really Mom?

Once I had my own place, my mom would come to my apartment to get rest from being out in those streets and to spend time with my baby and me. I was excited to build a relationship with her, so I was looking forward to her coming over when she did.

I remember I had picked her up from Vallejo because I just wanted to make sure that she was well. I used to worry a lot about her when she was in the streets. I wanted to feed her and let her take a hot bath and change her clothes. I drove around Vallejo hitting up the spots I knew she hung out at until I found her. Normally, if she weren't tired or was on one, she would be like "Come back to get me tomorrow, Tasha." But this time, she got in the car with no fight. I made sure that she was able to bathe and eat really well and be comfortable while she was with us. My son loved it when my mom would come over because she gave him whatever he wanted and let him do whatever.

The next day, we had woken up and planned to go grocery shopping together. So, as I was getting ready to go, I grabbed my purse to make sure that I had my stamps. Back then, they came in the books, so I was counting them to see how much I had. And I realized the big book I had was missing. She had seen me looking all over my room and the living room for them. So, she started helping me to look for them. I was getting frustrated because I did not have company and the only people that had been to my house were my sons' father and her. She asked me who had been to my house, and I told her the same thing; just her and my son's father. And she was like, "My child's father wouldn't steal from you." But at that moment, I thought maybe I just misplaced them. I never even had an inkling that she would have taken them. I ended up just going to the store with what I had. I was so mad that I could not find them.

My mom at the last minute said she didn't want to go to the store anymore. So, I just left her at my house. I left and came back, and she was gone. In my head, I was mad because this was my mother and I loved her to death and if she would have asked, I would have just given her the stamps not all of them but some of them. And for her to help me look for them knowing she had them the entire time, and she rather just left my house, just really hurt my feelings. But no matter what, if she called, I was going to come running.

When she came to my house, she didn't have nothing and back then you could go to the corner store and buy some cheap stuff and they gave you back real cash. And that's most likely how she was able to get back to Vallejo. I was just a broken girl who wanted her mom no matter what. She knew I was mad at her, so she didn't want to face me, which I knew she was going to run from me after that, because she didn't want to hear my words or see my hurt.

Life has taught me that heartache comes in many forms: family, lovers, friends, can break your heart. It's not an easy way to avoid, but it's possible.

Ways to Heal Heartache:

- *Make sure you create a routine. Take time to yourself go out to eat or get your nails done*
- *Ask for help if you have a support system*
- *Forgive yourself and learn when enough is enough*

Chapter 4

Surviving

I am not alone on my journey to healing in my soul. Others have walked it and come through victorious, and so will I!

– Joyce Meyers

I had my second son four years after my first child and his father was nothing like my first child's father. He came from a different background than me. His parents were still married and had been married his entire life. He didn't come from the struggle so to say. This was his first child. He kept a job, which is what I liked about him. We talked on and for off a minute. He ended up moving to Vegas. We continued our friendship, so he planned a trip for us to go visit right before Christmas time. He and his friend drove to pick us up. That was my first time ever visiting Vegas. When we started dating, I was trying to just get over my first son's father. I was young and still searching for a love in all the wrong places. I had no business being in another relationship, yet there I was. I ended up moving to Vegas and we got a place together.

I convinced my cousin, and her family to move there also. We were both staying with her mom at the time. So, we started searching for apartments and I found us some nice, cheap apartments. I had just gone to school for my medical assistant certification, and they had a lot of jobs in my field. I applied in my area and just was not having any luck finding anything. Although I was interning with Kaiser, due to the hiring freeze, I wasn't able to get hired on.

Then, things got real.

Life in Vegas

I lived in Vegas with my son's father for about a year. I was working in the medical field as a medical assistant in a small Obstetrics and gynecology office. They didn't pay as much as Cali due to the fact that the cost of living in Vegas was much cheaper. During this time is when I got pregnant with Keke. My cousin was pregnant, and we used to go to the swap meet there just to eat these spicy pickles and nachos. I didn't know I was pregnant too, which is why I liked the same food as she.

One night after I had got off work my legs and body were extremely sore. I charged it to a hard day of work and went to bed. The next day, I woke up for work and could not move out the bed to get up. I had to crawl to fix my baby his breakfast. The pain was so deep in my ankles and joints in my legs that the pain was too much to stand. I warmed a towel up in the microwave so that I could put it on my legs, hoping it would give me some comfort. I ended up going to the hospital and they of course said nothing was wrong and told me to take Tylenol. However, they recommended that I take a pregnancy test along with the blood work. The test was positive, and I was not expecting that at all.

Like at *all*.

I was nervous and scared; here I am, a young woman with one child and now about to bring another child in this world. I was not ready to be a mom again.

I had been dealing with being sick and barely able to care for my oldest son. I was trying to find out what was the root cause of it because every doctor I went to kept saying nothing was wrong with me. But I know my body. I knew something was wrong, which is why I kept going back so they can check me out.

It started right after I had my first son. I had lost a lot of weight and had little knots on my lower legs that were sore. My primary care doctor had referred me to a rheumatologist. They had run several different tests only to say that everything looked normal.

But I knew the amount of weight I had lost was not normal for me.

I was normally a size 7/8 and had gone down to a 0/1. I had been to so many different doctors, still, no one could tell me what was going on with me. I was so frustrated being told that nothing was wrong with me and not getting any answers that I had just learned to cope with the pain because I was tired of not getting any answers. I was drained, my body was sore, and I still couldn't figure out why I was so sick. I ended up losing my job because I couldn't walk and being sick. Soon after, I moved back to Cali pregnant and with a toddler.

Back To Cali

When I moved back to California, I wish I could say that things got better right away, but they didn't. I had got an offer to work at San Quentin as a Medical Assistant. Great!

However.

I didn't have a car to get there. So, guess who had to take the bus to drop her two toddlers off at daycare before catching the bus to work?

Yep.

You're probably thinking, Well what's so bad about catching the bus?

Well, my bus ride wasn't an easy route. I caught the bus to the daycare from home, which was not nearby. Then I would have to catch the bus from the daycare to another city. Then transfer to another bus that took me to San Quentin. That bus would drop me off at the end of the road. From there, I had to walk up this long road to get to the entrance of the prison.

So yes, doing that every day gets burned out quickly. It was a lot, but I was so happy to have gotten the job in the field that I went to school for. Eventually, I got support with dropping and picking the kids up. But then...

Not Everyone Supported, Though

During that time, my youngest son had gone with his father for the weekend. His dad lived with his mom and was not working at the time. I called and asked his father if he could keep him during the week until I was able to get a car. That way I wouldn't have to get the kids up so early. Plus, I was tired of getting on the bus with them. He agreed and then right after I hung up the phone, not even ten minutes later, and my phone rang, and it was Keke's grandmother. She was yelling on the phone saying that this is not her sons house and Keshawn could not stay there with him.

As the phone was to my ear, my aunt could hear yelling on my phone, and she saw my face in total disbelief. So, my aunt was asking me what was going on. I could not even get out what the grandma was saying because she was yelling so loud that my aunt heard her through the phone. So, my aunt took the phone from me to see what was going on. I was so mad, tears were flowing from my eyes. My aunt told her that she was wrong because that was her grandson and that I only asked so that I could go to work. The grandma tried to get fly with my aunt and my aunt told her she would whoop her ass and hung up on her.

They both worked at the same hospital together. So, it was definitely possible that my aunt would indeed whoop that ass. The grandmother must have thought about what my aunt said because she called back and tried to apologize to her. Not to mention, she still had my baby. She had to drop him off to me that day. So, she didn't want any problems!

I can laugh about it now, but it wasn't funny in the moment. That was a time I wish my mom were not in prison because she definitely would have had some choice words for her, and a fight would come with it. Well, maybe it was good that she wasn't around.

In that moment, I learned that support isn't owed, it's freely given. It made me appreciate those who support me genuinely even more. I told myself that I would never ever ask his father or grandparents for nothing ever in my life.

I knew I had to push through this rough patch no matter what. I knew that eventually, I would get a car and the stress of getting up super early, catching the bus in the cold with my babies was just temporary. So, I let that be my motivation as I pushed forward.

It All Gets Better

Working for the prison was actually one of my favorite jobs. I worked in the infirmary, which was the hospital/clinic for the prison. I met some cool people that I became close with. And we became close with a few of the correctional officers. They became like big brothers to us.

Soon after starting at the prison, I was able to move into my own place around the corner from my aunt in South Vallejo. One of the correctional officers saw me walking from the bus stop at the end of the road from San Quentin Prison and stopped and asked me if I wanted a ride. I said yes because I had talked to him a few times when he had come to get charts for a prisoner. Plus, the walk from where the bus let me off at was a far walk to the prison where we worked at. He said, "I know you don't catch the bus way from Vallejo to out here." I said, "Yes, I do I don't have a car right now, so I have to do what I have to do." He said, "Oh hell no! You do not have to do that." He said he also lived in Vallejo, and he didn't mind giving me a ride.

This was music to my ears. Before I got too excited, I asked him, "Are you sure?" in which he replied, "Girl yes, I'm sure. You are too fine to be traveling like that." I told him that I'll give him gas and he quickly said no like I offended him. He said, "I have to drive to work regardless, and you don't owe me anything."

That settled that. My aunty would pick the boys up and drop them off to daycare for a little bit. My mom ended up getting out of prison and came to live with me not long after I moved into my place. And she offered to watch the boys for me, so my aunt didn't have to pick up and drop them off anymore. Maleek had started pre-k at the school by my house and my mom would take him. Little did she know but she came back around in the nick of time.

That Old Thing Back

My youngest son's father ended up trying to make things work with us. And I was open to the idea of us being a family. So, I allowed him to come live with me. He proposed to me, and I accepted the proposal. I was excited even.

My mom bought my dress and his mother volunteered to help with the decorations. I'm sure it was only because she had invited her friends and family. I was still not too keen on her from the previous altercation we had. But me trying to be nice and not wanting to be disrespectful, I just didn't say much. I didn't mind her contributing, but I did not want her to help me plan my wedding.

Soon after the proposal, her true colors would show. All of the planning was basically being done by me and his mother, which I didn't feel comfortable with. I told him that and I felt ignored.

I mean, who am I marrying? You or your mother? He just didn't want anything to do with the wedding at all. He would leave with his homeboys, and I would ask him to take Keke and he didn't want to. I wouldn't have minded if his friends didn't have their kids around, but they did.

I started to feel stressed, and overwhelmed. The more I thought about everything, it just didn't sit well with me. I thought, "If it's going on like this before a wedding, a wedding will not change anything; it may get even worse."

I was starting to have regrets. The invites had already gone out. But I didn't care anymore. I knew that I couldn't go through with this wedding, let alone marriage. So, one day, I went to the library and typed up some postponed notes. I sent them to my friends and family. I just could not see myself getting married because he or his mom felt we needed to be married because we have a child together. My mind was made up and nobody could change it.

My mom called my phone shocked after she received her note. She asked, "Tasha you cancelled the wedding?" I told her, "Yes, because I'm not marrying anyone that barely takes care of his child while we are together and getting married won't make him do it either. Plus, it feels like I'm marrying the mom because she is the one planning most of the wedding." My mom told me that she understands my decision.

After I called the wedding off, seems like things got worse. I ended up getting laid off from San Quentin. Keke's dad moved back with his mother. And I'm back to being single, with no job.

I knew my mom was kind of mad only because she bought my dress, but she respected my choice to do what was best for me. After all, I am her one and only daughter and have my ways just like her.

I realized that the only reason I was going to marry my ex was out of survival mode. So many women do this and end up in failed marriages. One thing God taught me with this lesson is not to depend on no one but Him.

Keys to Surviving

- *Give yourself time and space to breath, but don't isolate yourself.*
- *In order to stay strong after a breakup you have to cut them off.*
- *Be positive and remember not every relationship will be the same*

Chapter 5

Unforgiveness

"Weeping may endure for a night, but joy comes in the morning."

Psalm 30:5

During this time in my life, my mom and I were trying to build our relationship. She got out of jail and said she was tired and really wanted to get herself clean for real. It was very hard for me to trust and believe her because I had heard this all my life from her. She would walk to her meetings from south Vallejo to Tennessee St and sometimes, they were at other locations. And if anybody knows, the walk is very far. But she was determined to get her life together like she said, and she used to say, "If you really want it, you will do whatever it takes to get sobriety." She would say, "Hell I used to walk for them drugs, so I got to walk to stay clean." At those moments, I still carried a lot of bitterness and hurt from her. In my head, I wanted to believe that she was truly serious this time but the other part of me said, "Yea she has said and did these things before and then eventually slipped back into her addiction." So, I tried not to get my hopes up too high like I've done in the past.

I used to know some of her triggers. In the past when she hung with certain people that she hung with when she smoked, she would end up back smoking. So, when she would be around those people, it made me second guess if she were serious. I had a lot of built-up anger that I held on to. And I would be so mad at her when she would hang with those people. She used to tell me "Tasha, if I'm going to smoke, it won't be because of who I hang with. I have a choice and if I choose to smoke, that is my choice, but I told you that I would not go back to that because I don't want my grandkids to see me like that." I still had my doubts, but I tried to believe even though that was something that I had been praying for all my life.

It kind of felt too good to be true. This last time after she went to prison and got out, she was definitely serious about staying clean. She kept her word and she started working as a drug and alcohol counselor. One of her first recovery jobs she had was with Shamia Recovery Center in Vallejo. It's crazy because she was once on the other end of it where she was the patient and now, she was the person helping those who walked the same path that she used to be in.

I have visited her at this same recovery center many times. She was very passionate about her job because she once was in the shoes of many of the ladies that she now helped to overcome addiction. A lot of the women she worked with loved her because she didn't play with them, but she would give them the shirt off her back. They knew they could not run circles or play games with her because she already knew all the games they would try to play before they even came to her.

Time For A Change

While I was so happy that my mom was clean and doing good with her life, I wasn't so happy with my own. I was still struggling, and I just didn't feel like myself anymore.

After getting laid off from San Quentin, I eventually decided to move to Texas with my boys. My aunt lived there with her family. She had been there for some years and her dad lived there and was from Texas. Whenever I talked to her, she would always try to get me to move there. She would tell me how cheap it was and how getting a job was very easy. After being tired of the California Chase, I ended up packing my belongings up and putting them in storage. I then moved to Texas in June of 2006. The only people that knew I was moving were my oldest son's grandparents. I didn't tell anybody that I was moving, not even my mom. I didn't want her or anyone else to try to talk me out of going.

I had needed a change to better my family and with all the things I heard about Texas, I figured why not give it a shot? My boys' fathers were not a consistent support in their lives, which is why I did not feel bad for going where I thought would be better for us. Had they been active figures in their lives, I would have reconsidered taking them so far away.

I stayed with my oldest son's aunt when I first moved to Texas. She and her husband had relocated there due to him being in the military. I did not stay with them for too long because I could not find a job where they lived. They lived in Killeen where most military families lived. I ended up moving to Austin and stayed with my aunt for a short time. I believe I moved there in the middle of July and had a job within that week and moved into my first apartment at the beginning of August. I had a 2-bedroom 1 bath for $600. Things were starting to look up, but not as fast or smoothly as I would have liked them to.

When I moved, I didn't have a car. So, I was getting on the bus with my kids doing what I had to do. I didn't have a babysitter at the time and was still waiting on my baby boy to get accepted into the daycare I had enrolled him in.

I kept job searching and finally got an interview, but still no babysitter. I really needed that job, so I decided to take him with me. I remember just praying to God telling him that I really needed that job and if it's for me, these people will look past me bringing my baby and give me this job. So, I held my head high and took my baby to my job interview.

When I got to the interview, it was a room full of people in the lobby waiting to be interviewed. I know they were looking at me like, "Why does she have this baby with her?" I didn't care. I confidently walked in there with my baby in his stroller.

I let the lady at the reception desk know that I was there for my interview, and I explained to her that I didn't have a babysitter, but I promised her that my baby would be quiet. Luckily, he was sleeping, and he had just fallen asleep from the ride on the bus to the job interview. The lady just looked, told me to sign my name in the sign in sheet and said to have a seat and she would let the interviewee know that I was there with my child. In my head, I thought, *I hope they still let me interview for this job.* Shortly, after I signed in, they called my name and a few other people that were in the lobby area.

As I walked into the interview, I saw that it was a group interview and not a one on one. I started to just leave but I walked in and had a seat. The first interviewee looked directly at me and said, "I know you are serious about this job because you brought your baby and didn't let it stop you from coming to this interview." At that moment, I could breathe. I was so nervous that they would tell me to come back when I could find a babysitter. But nope, they proceeded with the group interview, and I got the job.

God Favors Me

I've always been a go getter, but the way things lined up for me when I moved to Austin let me know that God favored me so much. I knew then that no matter the obstacle that came my way, I had to keep pushing.

Since I didn't have a car, I was blessed that my apartment was walking distance to and from the important places I needed to go: work, the kids daycare, grocery store. I would walk my oldest son to school. The bus stop was literally across the street from his school. So, after I would drop him off, I would catch the bus down the street to drop Keshawn off to daycare and the bus stopped right in front of his daycare. Then I would get back on the bus to go down a few more blocks to get to my job, of which the bus let me off a block before my job.

See how God showed out for me?

My apartment, the school, daycare, and my job were all off of the main road on Braker Rd. And I got up every day, even days when my body was in so much pain due to my Lupus, to make it happen. I was so used to dealing with the pain that nobody even knew I was suffering or in pain until I said something or had to go to the hospital to get steroid shots.

Battling with My Pain

I had battled with Lupus right after I had my oldest son, so it had been six years when I had moved to Texas that I had lupus. I had lost a lot of jobs because there were times that I just could not physically get to work. I would let my supervisors know that I battled with my condition but that didn't matter to them. I would have notes showing that I had gone to the ER due to my Lupus. I had tried to find a regular rheumatologist that could make this process with my job easier. I was referred to a doctor and when I went to her, she made me feel like I was lying about having lupus. She had my medical history charts from my California doctor but that still wasn't enough.

I absolutely loved my doctor in California. She was very helpful and genuine about the care for her patients. This new rheumatologist had me do blood work, and my labs came back normal. Despite the pain that I was in, she decided that I no longer had lupus. So, when I asked her, "Well, why am I having all these symptoms of a flare that I have battled with since being diagnosed with lupus in 2004?" She told me she does not know and all she can do is to give me some prednisone to help with the joint pain.

At this point, it brought back up the old memories of how long it took me to figure out that I had lupus. It was draining, stressful, and scary. I refused to have to walk down that same path where doctors acted like the things that I was experiencing were not true. One thing that I did miss about Cali was my doctor. She made sure to stay on me about making sure that I was covered in the summertime because the UV rays can trigger a lupus flare. And she didn't treat me like another number. She knew I had children and she would always tell me, "Your kids need you to be here on this earth with them so I will do everything to make sure that you're okay." And she would always tell me that you can live with lupus; it's not a death sentence. I used to wish I could just bring her with me.

So yes, when I left the doctor's office after that lady told me I didn't have lupus, I remember getting in my car and just crying. I was so frustrated, and I was in pain. Once I left, I told myself that I'm not going through the same thing I did before. It was pure hell. It took me almost four years to get my diagnosis.

So, I continued to remedy my own self when it came to my lupus flares. I knew if I ate any pork or peanuts, I would have a flare, so I stayed away from those two things. Stress caused a majority of my flares along with summertime heat. My joints would ache from time to time in the winter. But I had learned to cope with the pain.

The move to Texas was scary, especially since I really didn't have any family out there but still took the chance. I had days when I would be asking myself "Why in the heck did you move so far away?" But I actually loved Texas because the people were very helpful. I had met some people who would tell me about places that were hiring and very open to give information to help you out. People in Cali never wanted to give any information about anything. Everyone either didn't want you to get anything better than them or they just didn't care to share anything to help others.

Texas Changed My Life

Me moving to Texas made my mother and I's relationship so much better. She found out that I was out there by calling my aunt and my aunt told her she had seen me. My mom told her that she better take care of me even though I was grown. She was kind of sad that her grandbabies were far away from her. Anybody that knew her knew that she loved them to death. I called her a week after I got to Texas and explained to her why I didn't tell her I was leaving. She understood because she said she would have told me not to go but she knew I needed to do this for me.

We used to call each other all the time after work and during work. Just talking about her job or I would be telling her about how the kids were doing; or if I was feeling stressed out paying childcare and bills etc. She always knew just what to say to make me feel better. She never forgot to tell me how good of a mother I was and that all my hard work would pay off. She didn't always have the answer to fix the problem, but she made sure to encourage me to keep my head up and keep pushing for my babies.

Hearing her say she loved me and that she was proud of me was better than anything in the world. I had longed to have that mother and daughter relationship that we were building. My sons loved their Nana, as they called her, and she could do no wrong in their eyes at all. If they called and asked for anything, you best believe they got it. The things that she could not do for me and my brother, she made up with her grandkids and I loved that about her.

Getting My Groove Back

I had started dating a guy that I met in Texas; he was in the military. I met him through my oldest son's aunt's husband. They were having a barbeque one weekend. I lived in Austin, TX and they lived in Killeen, TX which is an hour drive. I didn't have a car at the time, so her husband came to pick us up. Not knowing he had already told his friend about me and had him drive down with him to pick me and the boys up. I had no intentions of dating because I was just trying to get myself together and established. While we were in Killeen at the kickback, he made sure that he wasn't leaving without getting my number. We all had a good time, and everyone was kicking back and talking. He seemed like a cool dude. We continued to converse for some weeks before we actually went on a date.

On our first date, he took me and the boys to this kid's amusement park. He knew I had kids and he knew that I was with them full-time, so he knew I was a package deal. I liked that about him, especially since he didn't have any kids. We started dating soon after and next thing I know, I'm in love. Well, at least I think it's love.

There I was, young, naïve, and wanting to be loved. Empty, thinking a man should be the one to fill me up. Not even knowing how to truly love myself. I thought having a man would fill that void. It was so easy to love him. He was stable, attentive, and cared for me and the boys. We spent lots of time together, so I felt safe with him. He and my boys had built a close bond. Things were going really good between us and before I knew it, I ended up getting pregnant.

But was in denial.

I remember he kept telling me, "You're pregnant," and I would tell him, "No the hell I'm not!" He kept saying, "You need to go take a test," and I just brushed it off. I finally went to the doctors and sure enough, I was pregnant. I called my mom crying. "What am I going to do with three kids?" I thought about having an abortion but deep inside, I knew I could not go through with killing my baby. My mom told me, "Girl, you are not having any abortion and don't be worrying about anything because as long as I'm living, your kids will be good, boo."

I called him after my doctor's appointment to tell him. All he said was, "I already knew you were." It's crazy because I was not sick prior to my appointment then right after it was confirmed I started being so sick and nauseated.

This pregnancy for me was way different then my two prior pregnancies. I was not sick at all with my boys. I craved cherries and was so drained with this pregnancy. The job that I had required me to work overnight and when I got off, I had to get the boys ready. That schedule had my body all out of whack because I was so fatigued due to my Lupus and being drained from my pregnancy. I would get my rest in after I dropped my boys off and then I had to be back up around 2:45 pm to pick them up from school and daycare.

I had been saying I wanted a girl so bad and now I was having one.

My daughter's father would come down to help me out with the boys during the week when he could and every weekend.

Okay, here's my little drama. So, my daughter's father was in the process of getting a divorce from his wife when we met and so, well. I guess you can see how things were a little complicated.

What Had Happened Was

Okay, so yes, he was married, but separated. So, in my eyes, it was okay to continue seeing him. I believed what he said because he had his own place that he shared with one of his military buddies. I know I probably should not have messed with him until his divorce was final but hey! It be like that sometimes. I've forgiven myself for it.

Now, to my understanding, the marriage was over, but there was one particular time that made me feel otherwise. My oldest son's aunt had a gathering and invited me and my daughter's father. We kept seeing this car drive up and down the street with a car full of females. We didn't really pay too much attention to the car until they kept coming back. We were all drinking so we looked at the car with suspicion. My ex and I ended up leaving there and went to his house not knowing the entire time that we were being followed by his soon to be ex-wife. She knew where my son's aunt lived but did not know where my ex lived, from what he told me. So, she saw my car and made sure to follow us to his house.

Tia, and his homeboy stayed over with us at his house. His homeboy was in the living room of the house. My car was parked right in front of his house. I woke up to a lady busting in his room yelling at my ex, "Who is this?" He was knocked out asleep because the night before, we were all partying and wasted from drinking and having a good time. I had no clue who she was, but something in my gut told me this is the wife. I had never seen her or met her but I'm sure it's her.

As she was questioning him, I start putting my shirt and some pants on while she was on his side of the bed. She slapped him awake and he jumped up startled from her yelling. He got out the bed and put on his sweats. He then told her to get out his house and mentioned that he didn't have to answer to what she was talking about because they were not together. Tia was in the extra room sleeping but she heard all the commotion, and she came out the room. His homeboy who let the wife just walk in the door because he didn't lock it from the night before was sitting on the couch like nothing was going on. When the wife walked in the house, she came to the first room she saw. And instead of the homeboy checking her at the door, he sat on the couch and didn't do shit. So as the wife was steady going off and wouldn't leave out the house, he finally put her out his house himself. She ended up coming back and then came to me to ask who I was. I told her "Don't question me about shit." I guess that triggered her because she started to come towards me and before I knew it, Tia was walking up to her saying 'Bitch you better back up off my sister" and tagged her ass a few times.

That still didn't stop her; she backed up a little and then continued to come at me again. And that's when I charged her ass. Before I could really get her good, he had grabbed her and put her out his house.

During this time, I didn't know I was pregnant. So, me, my daughters father and Tia were outside and the soon to be ex-wife had gone to her car and then came back to the porch. She still was trying to figure out who I was. She said, "Did he tell you I was pregnant?" and I just looked at him like, *oh really.* He pleaded to me that she was lying and that she wasn't pregnant. I didn't know who to believe. He was saying one thing but I'm thinking, "Why would she be saying that? It has to be some truth to it." But later, he insisted that they had been separated and he didn't mess with her at all because she was sleeping around with other men in the military. She was also in the military, and I believed him because we were together all the time.

Or so I thought.

At the time of the altercation with his ex, I had no idea that I was pregnant. I found out a few weeks after this incident. I also later found out she was not lying. Her child was supposed to be born in December but was born early; she had him in November 2007. I had my baby girl in February 2008.

Even after she had the baby, my child's father still didn't believe her baby was his and they had a DNA test. The baby came out to be his. He claims he went by her house to record her telling on herself about sleeping with other men so that he wouldn't have to pay spousal support. And he did show me the videos and he claimed that she took advantage of him while he was drunk and that's how the baby came about.

I found out about all of this after we went our separate ways.

The Princess Is Here

Now, life wouldn't be life if it didn't get worse before it got better, right?

Well, soon after I found out that I was pregnant, he was soon to be deployed to Iraq. He also had got in some trouble with the law, and he thought he was going to be going away to do a lot of time. He wanted me to consider about having an abortion because he said he didn't want to have a child that he would not be able to care for financially and physically. I couldn't believe he even had the audacity to even suggest such a thing. I told him I was not having an abortion and I would take care of my baby by myself if I had to. I ended up shutting down from him completely. I wasn't answering his calls or calling him at all. He ended up getting deployed. And I moved back to California with my mom right before I was scheduled to have my baby girl.

I was scheduled to have a c-section February 20, 2008. I had an emergency c-section with my oldest son due to being in labor for three days and the stress of if caused his heart rate to go up. And my doctor informed me that because I have big kids and I was so petite, I had the option to have natural labor, but she said most likely, I would end up having to have a c-section anyway.

After having my oldest, I opted to have c-sections with my youngest son and my baby girl. My mom was right by my side the day when I went in to have my baby girl. We had to be at the hospital at 6am that morning to get prepped for the c-section. I was scheduled to have my tubes tied after I delivered as well.

While I was lying on the surgery table while the doctors were cutting me, I felt pressure on my stomach. And then my doctor said, "She's here." My mom was sitting next to me at the head of the table. The doctor asked my mom if she would like to cut the umbilical cord and my mom got up to go cut it. Then they brought my baby girl to me so I could see her. I could not hold her because I was still in surgery. So, my mom placed her close to my face so I could kiss her little cheeks; she was wrapped up like a little butterfly cocoon.

Right, after I kissed my baby, I heard my doctor tell the other doctors "She can still hear you." And after that, I don't remember anything until I woke up that evening tied to the bed and intubated.

I later found out that as my doctor was in the process of tying my tubes, I started bleeding out. My lupus and the medications I was taking made my blood really thin. I had to get a blood transfusion and I had coded three times. I had to end up having a hysterectomy in order to save my life. I had gone into surgery at around 6:30 am and I delivered my baby at around 8:30 am. I was in surgery from the time I delivered until around 1 or 2pm.

My mom said she was a nervous wreck because after she let me kiss my baby, she ended up going in the other room with the nurse to wash up my baby and feed her. So, she just thought they were finishing up stitching me up after my delivery. Until, she said hours had passed and nobody had come to get her to come see me. She had asked the nurses and they said they couldn't tell her anything due to confidentiality. My mom's oldest sister worked at the same hospital that I delivered at downstairs. So, my mom went to see if my aunt could find out what was going on. But of course, they couldn't tell her anything either.

When I coded, they announced it over the intercom of the entire hospital, so my aunt had heard it but did not know it was me. They had to just wait until someone came to give them information. My mom said all she could do was pray. She said she kept getting phone calls asking how I was doing. And said she was ready to break down because she didn't even have a clue what was going on. And she said she was like, "What am I going to do with three kids if something happened to Tasha?" We laughed about it when she was telling me the story once I was out of ICU.

I had finally gotten my girl, so I was done at this point, and I wasn't disappointed that I had a hysterectomy. I knew from that point that God had something in store for me. I could have easily died during childbirth, but God kept me for a reason.

My child's father ended up getting in contact with me a few weeks after I had my baby. And he told me that he was glad I did not listen to him and had my baby. He asked if I could send him some pictures because he was still in Iraq. And he said whatever she needed, he would get it, which she didn't need much because I had already everything except her crib.

I was living with my mom but was moving to my own apartment within a few weeks. So, he ordered her the crib that I picked out. I remember when he called back after seeing her pictures; I could hear the excitement in his voice when he talked about her. This was his first child that got to be in his life. The child from his ex-wife, she did not allow him to see him at all. And they were not on good speaking terms since the divorce was final. I made sure to send him pictures for him to keep up with her different stages of life since he was gone.

This phase of my life taught me all about forgiveness. When you hold on to pain or disappointment, you block future blessings. If I held on to unforgiveness, I wouldn't have had my mom to support me giving birth to my kids. My daughter wouldn't know her father. It took me a while, but forgiveness saved me.

Ways to Heal Unforgiveness

- *The first step in healing from unforgiveness is to acknowledge the hurt*
- *Then accept that you cannot change the past.*
- *Don't pretend like you have forgiven when you really have not. Decide if you are going to forgive*

Chapter 6

Resilience

"What comes easy won't last, and what
lasts won't come easy."

- Author Unknown

Starting from a young girl, I was searching for love that I hadn't received from my parents. I would look for love of a mother in older women that I had become close to. And I was looking for the love of a father in men that I dated. I had been hurt so much that I became numb to it and moved from one hurt to the next. Dealing with my relationships with my kids fathers as well. Once I started having my kids, it was no longer about me or what I was dealing with. I had to go into survival mode. So, any emotions or feelings I had dealing with the pain, I suffered with in silence. I held everything in and then when I would get overwhelmed with life and being a single mother. I would breakdown in private and then push it aside and continue taking care of everyday things. I never dealt with the issues at hand, which caused me to have not so good parenting skills as far as learning to control my temper when I was frustrated by life issues.

My kids could do something wrong that I had repeatedly asked them to correct over and over, like cleaning up. I would blow up and yell at them. I would be stressed out about something else like how I was going to pay childcare expenses. And that one little thing would just make me explode.

My ideal life was never to be a single mother but those were the cards that I was dealt. I didn't want anyone to feel sorry for me or feel like I was a burden, so I dealt with anything that I was going through on my own. I was angry with my kids' fathers for not being consistent figures in their lives and leaving me to figure it all out. I don't regret having my kids at all; they made me the woman that I am today. However, having three kids who depend on you for everything can be hard at times.

As a mother, I didn't have the option to give up at all. There were days when I had to push myself through the pain, and sickness of my Lupus to still be present for my kids and also work to put food on the table and a roof over their heads. One of the triggers to my Lupus flares was stress. And I believe that played a major part of my illness at the time. But one thing I knew to do when nothing else seemed to work was to pray. I believe prayer carried me through many of my tough days when I felt like I wasn't going to make it.

The relationship that my mom had with all three of my children was like none other. I was glad that they were all so close and that they never got to experience the old person that she was. I loved seeing how they interacted together. I barely could tell them anything without her ready to knock me out. If they called, she was running. There were times, I would pray to God to get my mother clean, he had finally answered my prayers and I will forever be grateful. It wasn't on my time but on hers. She had to be ready to do it on her own time. Yes, I was a grown child once she got fully clean and off drugs but the beauty in it was that she was an amazing grandmother. And her grandkids just knew her as Nana who got them whatever they wanted. She would take them to her NA meeting, and they would come back home telling me they got to make their own coffee and tea. I would tell them "Yawl did not need no dang coffee and I'm sure yawl poured all the sugar there was in it." They all would laugh, and she would just say "Tasha, they are fine." She let them do whatever they wanted, and they knew it.

My goal when I moved to Texas was to get established to purchase a house so that my mom could move here with us. And then I planned to buy her a house to stay in. I wanted to be able to get us both setup in Texas. She used to tell me that if I found her a job there, she would come but she wanted to stay in the same field she was in which was being a drug and alcohol counselor.

I know she wanted to be close to us because then she would be able to see her grandkids more often than just the summertime. She had my kids spoiled rotten. I ended up moving back to Texas when Nevaeh was about 1 years old. I loved my hometown, but it was no support besides my mom or anything to help people there. And it was hard to find a good job in Cali.

The thing I loved about Texas was that it was easy to get a good job. And they had so many resources for single mothers. I knew that if I stayed in Cali, I would be on government assistance with a low paying job, barely getting by unless I had section 8 or subsidized apartments. Of which, I was living in a 3-bedroom subsidized townhome in Suisun. I was paying $100 because I was not working and was getting government assistance at the time, which some would say that was good but when you're only getting $400-500 a month on top of having to pay lights, car insurance and diapers, wipes, and other basic essentials; you are basically left with cheap rent and no money.

I knew I didn't want to live the rest of my life like that. So, I mustered up the strength to do what I had to do for my kids. Best choice ever.

Ways to Become Resilient

- *Prov 3:5 "Trust in the Lord with all your heart, and do not lean on your own understanding"*
- *Pray even when you do not understand.*
- *I knew that if I prayed and asked for help, he would carry me through*

Chapter 7

Grief

"Tears are part of the process of healing in our soul."

-Author Unknown

I thought I had been through some of the most painful things in my childhood. Until the day I lost my mother to cancer in 2011. That was one of the most painful things I have ever endured in life. There was one thing that I had been praying and asking God to do in my life which was to get my mother cleaned up off of drugs. He did grant my wish. Not on my time, but His. She was first diagnosed with cancer in 2010. Prior to her diagnosis, she had, had an abnormal pap which she never went back to get it checked. And her doctor had finally convinced her to come in and get a recheck. That's when they discovered she had cervical cancer.

At that time, it wasn't that bad. So, her doctor scheduled for her to have surgery to remove it. She had called me one day after work to let me know about her having cancer, but she was having surgery and her oldest sister was going with her. She had planned to just have her surgery and then tell me about it afterwards. She didn't want me to be stressed out or sick. One of her co-workers told her that she should not wait to tell me because if something happened in surgery, I would be mad. Her coworker was right. I would have been pissed had she not told me prior to her surgery.

My mom ended up coming to visit me and the kids for the first time ever in Texas, since she had time off from her surgery. I don't know who was more excited to finally get her to come see us: my babies or myself. She was able spend time with us and her baby sister as well. I moved back to Cali some months after because I was having a hard time with the cost of childcare for my baby girl. And my mom told me to just come back home, which I'm glad I did because that gave us time together.

My mom's cancer had come back in full force in 2011. She was having symptoms of a bad cough. And thought it was due to her smoking cigarettes or possibly dust at her job. She ended up going to the doctors and they did an X-ray. It didn't show anything. So, my aunt Val, who is her older sister, told her to make them do a CAT scan. Not long after the CAT scan, her doctor called and told her to come in for an appointment.

It was in April of 2011. I remember because it was a day before my oldest son's birthday. My mom, my aunt Val, I and my baby girl went to her doctor's appointment. Her oncologist doctor pulled up her CAT scan on a TV monitor and it showed nothing but spots all over the screen. The doctor began to explain what we saw. He said that the cancer had come back. That it had spread everywhere, including her blood stream. He then told my mother that she had two options: one was to do chemo and radiation treatment, or the other was to give her medicine to make her comfortable during her last days. He told her that she had six months to live and asked what she wanted to do.

With tears falling down her face, my mom told him she wanted to live to see her grandkids graduate.

I remember hearing those words from the doctor saying she only had six months to live, and it stung bad.

After begging God to deliver my mother from drugs, now I have to hear she is dying. I was numb and in shock. I believe we all were in shock. The doctor took her off of work from that day forward. She had been working up until that doctor's visit. Her health deteriorated and she ended up in the hospital soon after that.

Preparing For The Worst

During that time, the nurse had advised both of us to go over her action plan as far as if things turned for the worst-case scenario. My mom made me power of attorney over her. And she was still legally married but had been separated from her husband for years. She told the nurse that he did not have any power or say at all when it came to her. She said, "My daughter is the only one that has power to make shots if I'm not able to do so myself." The nurse had us both sign forms stating that was my mom's wishes as far as who could make choices on her behalf.

My mom was well known and so she had so many visitors when she was in the hospital. I remember coming to visit her after she had just had a big group of people visiting. And I told her, "If you end up in here and cannot speak for yourself, I am not allowing all these folks be to visiting you until you get better." Some of her visitors were just coming to be nosey. Then it was a rumor that she was back smoking crack because she had lost so much weight due to the cancer. And that really made me angry with some of her so-called friends. Anybody in their right mind could see she was sick. She had lost all her hair from chemo and radiation. She started laughing and was like, "I know missy pooh. I know you going to make sure that I'm taken care of."

Every time I would ask her wishes, she told me she didn't want to talk about it, which I didn't either honestly so I left her alone about it. It would be times when she just wanted to get out the house so I would take her to Trans and get her fried shrimp, which was her favorite. And then she would to go to her friend, Brenda's house.

One particular day while hanging out at Brenda's, things turned for the worst. I took her over there one day and we were all sitting in the garage talking. She ended up in ICU mid-July and passed away August 19, 2011. I was right next to her every day up until she took her last breath.

It Hurts So Bad

On that day, she took half of my soul with her when she left this earth. I was disappointed with God. I didn't understand how he could give me a glimpse with her as my mother and then snatch her right back from me. I'm grateful for the seven years that he let me share with her without her being addicted on drugs. But I felt my heart and air in my body was ripped from my body when I lost her; my mother, my best friend, my kid's grandmother, the only women who knew me better than anyone else. I had to watch her suffer during her battle with cancer. I would hear her crying herself to sleep at night, and not being able to fix her problem hurt me so bad. She had already suffered so much in life and here she was fighting for her life not only for herself but for me as well. I had begged her to keep fighting one day when we went to one of her doctor's appointments. She had come out from one of her doctor's visits in her wheelchair and she instantly started crying and told me she was tired. And I broke down with her and begged her to keep fighting.

If I could have carried her pain, I would have.

I'm not even going to lie, I was angry and hurt after my mother died. I was mad at God because all those times I had prayed for her to get free from drugs and then He turned right around and took her from me. I felt like I was getting the one thing I had prayed for my entire life. And then it was just snatched from me in a blink of an eye.

I questioned how He could let someone who He said He loved to suffer so much throughout her life. I wondered if God really loved me like He said He did. All my life, I had prayed for the moment I could be with my mom and even though it wasn't until I was an adult, I still was happy to have my mom free and clean of drugs. Her death affected me tremendously. I was a dead man walking. I was only surviving because of my kids.

There were so many times I thought about if they would be better off without me because of the pain I was causing them due to my own pain that I was dealing with. I was always yelling and just angry. I didn't have anyone that I could talk to because no one truly understood the hurt and pain that I was dealing with.

Taking Responsibility For My Pain

One day, I got tired of feeling dead inside and that's when I told myself right before my fortieth birthday, I needed to get help and start my healing process. I started therapy and was able to get out some things that I had buried inside. I also prayed and asked God to help me with my healing and forgiveness.

Healing is not an overnight fix but every day, I have to show up and choose happiness over everything. Don't get me wrong, I have my days when I feel like I want to go back into that black hole. And when I feel like that, I pray and seek God even more. And He gives me so much peace.

I sometimes question how I got here. I know it's by the grace of God. He has and will always carry me through even when I couldn't see for myself. I honestly feel like with everything I went through as a child, God was preparing me for my latter days.

Had I not been that strong woman, I would have given up so easily to addiction or suicide by not being able to handle all of the things that life threw at me. I want the women who may be reading my story to know not to ever give up even when they cannot see the light at the end of the tunnel. It may not feel good when you are going through things, but God will always be there to catch you when you fall. He will carry you when you cannot carry yourself.

I look back over my life and know that nobody, but God was able to get me through the good and bad times that I've had.

I'm glad that I was able to enjoy my mom while she was clean for seven years out of my life. I miss having our mom and daughter dates; or even calling her to vent about my kids or anything. She may not have been able to fix anything, but just hearing her say, "Tasha, you are a damn good mom and I'm so proud of you." Just those words alone would fix anything.

At times, I feel cheated because I only got to have her for a short time but at the same, I'm thankful, because I could have lost her in her addiction without even getting a chance to chill and hang with her in her right state of mind. So, getting to see her clean herself up and live in the same city she used to get high in, and staying clean, as well as helping other addicts until she took her last breath was a blessing.

Four Phases of Grief

When I lost my mom, I learned about something called the four phases of grief. It explains what happens to someone who is grieving the loss of a loved one. Here are the phases.

Shock and Numbness: This phase immediately follows a loss to death. In order to emotionally survive the initial shock of the loss, the grieving person feels numb and shut down.

Yearning and Searching: This phase is characterized by a variety of feelings, including sadness, anger, anxiety, and confusion. The grieving person is experiencing a longing for the deceased person and wanting them to return to fill the emptiness created by their death.

Disorganization and Despair: This phase is marked by initial acceptance of the reality of the loss. The grieving person may experience feelings of apathy, anger, despair, and hopelessness. The person often desires to withdraw and disengage from others and the activities they regularly enjoyed.

Reorganization and Recovery: In the final phase, the grieving person begins to return to a new state of "normal." Intense feelings such as sadness, anger, and despair begin to diminish as more positive memories of the deceased person increase. The person may experience regular energy levels and weight will stabilize (if it fluctuated during other phases).

The main phase that I found myself stuck in was yearning and searching. I felt so empty, and I never thought I would come out of this phase. I did not start accepting her being gone until I started seeing my therapist and talking about it. I never got to truly grieve her and talk about my feelings until then. Before she passed, I was her caretaker and could not allow her to see me weak. Then when she passed, I had to jump back into mama mode.

So, to anyone who has lost a loved one seek help if you feel like you're not okay. You need to allow yourself to properly grieve.

Ways to Heal Grief

- *Talk about the good times you shared with your loved one*
- *Remember it's okay to feel sad and cry sometimes*
- *Never allow anyone to tell you how you should grieve.*

Chapter 8

Living

"Change isn't easy and is often painful, we have only two choices- the endure the pain of change or to endure the pain of never changing."

– *Unknown*

When I first started my healing journey, I thought it would be a quick fix; not knowing healing takes time. If you have endured so much pain over a decade, there is no way you can be fixed with a snap of a finger. Healing will not take place until honesty does. Once I became honest with myself, I could feel some things falling off. And when I say being honest with myself, I mean I had to let some things go and really forgive. I also had to admit that I had issues that needed to be fixed. I was still holding on to everything that had hurt me in my past: my mother, my father, my kids' fathers, friends, and some family. Those things were causing me to not trust, not to love, and to keep my guard down around people that have never hurt me. And it did not feel good being broken inside.

People only saw the pretty smile or me laughing to cover up the brokenness that I was hiding from everyone. I knew I had to dig deep within and admit that I was not okay.

And it's okay to not be okay.

I was so used to having to be strong because being strong was the only cards I was dealt. And I knew I did not want my kids to have to go through anything I've been through. So, I had to fix me in order to be a healthy mother mentally for my children.

I know I have made some mistakes as a mother. And I have apologized to my children because I want them to know that yes, I love them, but I have made mistakes that I am not proud of. I believe that holding on to un-forgiveness and all my other past trauma's caused a lot of my health issues with lupus. Once I started being real with myself and started working on a better Tasha, my health began to get better, and my lupus is currently in remission since 2019.

I realized pent-up feelings are harmful and need to be released. Stuffing or suppressing our feelings can also cause physical problems such as sleep troubles and digestive issues.

As a young girl I use to want to go to different drug rehabs and talk to the young girls of addict's children. I used to think about it all the time. And now I feel like sharing my story in some way give women a sense of hope. I want women to know that no matter what struggles they grew up in they did not have to be a product of their environment.

When I say that *I Am Healed* I'm simply saying I'm no longer allowing my past to dictate my future. I'm not allowing my old junk to take root in my head any longer. I am letting it all go. I have let those old things go and live in the present.

I cannot change my past, and somehow God felt like I was strong enough to handle the cards I was dealt. I now know that my story was not for me but to help someone else.

I am free to be happy, I am free to love myself, I am free to forgive myself, and I am free to live.

I do not want to give you false hope, so I will openly tell you that if you have been hurt, abandoned, rejected, or wounded through long-term illness or disappointments in life, your journey to healing will not be easy, but it will be worth it. The reason it is not easy is that you will have to open up areas of your life that you may have kept hidden or stuffed somewhere deep inside you.

The key to living is being honest with yourself. My healing has been constant because of my choice to live in truth. My prayer is that you too embrace your truth so that you may be healed.

"Only the truth will set us free but facing that truth may be one of the most difficult things we ever do." - Joyce Meyer

Keys to Living

- *Live your life unapologetically.*
- *Don't apologize for putting yourself first.*
- *Your purpose in life is to find your purpose and give your whole heart and soul to it*

I Am Healed

About the Author

Tasha Moneek is a mom of three, an advocate for women, and an author. The Solano County native is passionate about encouraging women to address their trauma, and take the necessary steps to properly heal their emotional wounds. In her debut book, *I Am Healed,* Tasha transparently shares the journey she took as she maneuvered through life's hardships, adjusted to being a single mother, and courageously released her past baggage. Her hope is for women to find their own courage to embrace transformation and a fresh start. She plans to use her platform to inspire other women who are having a cocoon experience to remain encouraged and continue growing into the butterfly she's intended to be.

I Am Healed